Table of Contents

Published 2009 as Ebook and 2011 as paperback
by Innovative Leadership International LLC

ISBN-13: 978-1461110491
ISBN-10: 1461110491

This publication is designed to provide accurate and authoritative information with regard to the subject matter covered. It is sold with the understanding that neither the author nor the publisher is engaged in rendering legal, accounting, or other professional service. If legal advice or other expert assistance is required, the services of a competent professional person should be sought.

—From a Declaration of Principles jointly adopted
by a Committee of the American Bar Association
and a Committee of Publishers and Associations

Ebook formatting and cover design by Exceptional Business Solutions, Inc.
Book design and formatting by Sandra Larson Design

Available through SuziPomerantz.com

Introduction

The global economy has changed everything. The game is different in the Age of Social Media because now it's not enough to have great business cards and go to networking meetings, smile and shake a few hands, meet and greet a few movers and shakers, practice the old elevator pitch. We have to be visible and engaged on Linked In, Facebook and Twitter. We have to engage people on a blog. We have to manage our online reputation. We have to network internationally and in multiple platforms simultaneously. We have to network ALL THE TIME! Networking is not what we thought it was just a few short years ago. Coaching is one of those businesses where regardless of whether you sell B2B or B2C, your networking skills are now as critical if not more so than your coaching skills. Leadership requires mastery of networking and social media with a strategic understanding of how they intersect so that you can effectively lead your team, employees, volunteers, or coaching clients.

NOW WHAT?!

Relax, I'm here to help. This eBook was created in response to the changing face of networking, especially to help you learn to navigate the new landscape easily so that you can focus on what you do best, which is coach your clients and lead your business!

This eBook will cover the basic mindsets of real life networking, and show you how to leverage and integrate those mindsets and practices into social networking online. The good news is that you are not alone. The better news is that you don't have to figure it out all by yourself or reinvent any wheels. This handy little guide will show you the fun and easy way to get your networking game on and play with the free tools available in order to grow your leads, prospects, clients, and ultimately your profits.

THE CATCH...

Of course, you will have to bypass your fears, concerns, and doubts about your capacity to network like a pro and expand your confidence and competencies in the direction of your ideal vision for your coaching practice/coaching business. You will have to get in

www.SuziPomerantz.com

the game because this is a sport with no bench. You will probably have to let go of a few limiting beliefs about how it should be. And in order to succed you will have to lighten up and have fun. Yes, you must enjoy yourself. So there.

YOU CAN DO IT!

Lots of folks are coaches these days, have you noticed? While it may be easy to become a coach, getting your calendar filled with coaching clients is a skillset often overlooked by most of the coach training programs out there. Of course, you can always use the book *Seal the Deal* as your business development training, but Networking is the critical first step and the go-to action for starting, growing, and unsticking your coaching business. When I wrote *Seal the Deal*, social media hadn't yet exploded onto the scene and there is nothing in that book about this incredibly important busines development opportunity! That's why I'm releasing this eBook. We've excerpted some of the best core concepts on networking from *Seal the Deal*, updated it, revised it, improved it, re-worked it, and added to the topic so that you can quickly get rocking in social media with ease and joy.

Nothing in here is rocket science, so jump in and get yourself wet. Try out variations and find your natural style with all the suggested activities so that your personality can shine through. Introverts and extroverts alike can benefit from the suggestions in this eBook, and one of the key success strategies for all of the networking platforms is an attitude of play and of *being yes*.

Being Yes is as simple as going into every conversation with a yes. Not a "yes, but...", just a simple "yes". It is remarkable what shifts in your process from that point on. It is a matter of self-leadership. If you can cause your attitude and mindsets to align with YES, knowing and trusting that you will solve all the problems of resources when and if they arise, you have much more freedom and latitude to generate new opportunities.

Being Yes is the secret to proactive growth in your business. Don't worry about the how or the when, just be a yes and it will happen!

Networking is no longer something you do when you are thinking about growing your business. Networking in the age of social media means that you have the opportunity to be plugged in 24/7 and if you are not taking advantage of that opportunity you are leaving money on the table.

Now, let's get to it shall we?

What Is Networking?

In the purest sense of the word, it is what you are doing anytime you are creating a genuine human connection with another person with no particular agenda in mind; only the joy of exploring what's possible between the two of you. What can we make happen? What do we have in common? What can we learn from each other? How can we play together? It is the relational aspect of your business. It is connecting with others to share resources, information, leads, referrals, ideas, and so on. Cultivating a working network of relationships is crucial to your business development system. Networking is about connecting, meeting people, collecting people. You are networking when you are:

- Building your pipeline

- Connection-seeking with genuine interest in others

- Meeting people

- Talking to people and getting to know them better

- Getting out there and creating relationships of all kinds

- Asking to meet other people -- asking for introductions or at least requesting contact information and permission to use your contact as a reference

- Following up with someone you met in passing

- Applying or improving your manners, etiquette, and social graces

- Introducing people to each other with an eye to expanding others' networks

- Engaging in activities that yield human connection and interaction, not necessarily related to business

- Keeping in mind the Nine Mindsets of Networking

- Finding out what people do, where they do it, why they do it and what they want to do

- Interacting with people in a way that generates relatedness.

- At any social event

- Out in the world in any way that has you interact with other people: think grocery store, picking up kids from school, attending local events, etc.

I particularly like the way Mary Foley describes it:

"Knowing how to network well can make or break your career. That's how powerful it is, because that's how powerful relationships are to your career. I'm not keen on the term "networking". The problem is the word "work". I mean how many times do you walk into a room full of people expecting to leave with actual work in hand such as a signed contract? It doesn't happen! Why? Because before someone signs their name or hands over a check, there's lots of getting to understand each other, lots of exchange, and making a connection. So, I say we rename "networking" to "netconnecting". Meeting and getting to know new people is about gathering – netting – several good connections. Once you've connected, sharing business cards is simply the convenience of not having to write down their contact information on a napkin."

Networking is more than just netconnecting, though. It is more like netweaving, because you've got to weave together your connections –– perhaps we should call it netknitting, because you are knitting together people and resources and ideas for everyone's mutual benefit. The more you can think in terms of weaving or knitting, the less working you'll have to do!

Networking is the backdrop of the sales process. It informs your strategic target choices, it lubricates the wheels of progress, it cultivates the garden of possible leads. And you'll make lots of new friends!

If you work in an organization, networking becomes even more critical in learning how to build coalition and influence results in your organization or department or team.

Leadership requires powerful partnerships. Knowing how to network will give you access to generating and sustaining powerful partnerships.

Being good at what you do isn't enough these days. Internal politics and the art of building powerful partnerships and relationships allows you to become the driver of your own career, which is the ultimate job security!

All of my coaching work with executives and leaders happens at the intersection of leadership and business development. Your leadership effectiveness, and your effectiveness as a coach, depends on your ability to successfully engage, enroll, build coalition, influence others, socialize ideas, and master self-leadership to really make things happen in your organization. Of course a lot of this is going to be dependent on your organization's particular culture, and your ability to navigate the political landscape in which you work. Success is effortless when you leverage the ways in which your leadership skills and your coaching skills are intertwined with your business development skills.

It is just as important to think strategically about internal business development as a critical function of your role as leader as it is for an organization to think about biz dev as a means to a robust bottom line. The people in your organization, all around you, will need to be engaged in your biz dev activity. Results happen in conversation, would you agree with that?

You are already always in either a networking, marketing or selling conversation in your job at work. You may not have articulated it quite that way, but think about it. It's how things get done in organizations. Your ability to bring creativity and leverage to influencing, engaging, motivating others, effectively communicating your ideas and programs, seeking buy in from your c-suite, from your direct reports, from your board, from your customers, from any of your constituents, requires biz dev awareness and capacity. Networking internally is how you increase visibility, sell ideas, and lead through influence. When you are visible, connected, and effectively networked in your organization and your industry, you become irreplaceable in your organization.

       www.SuziPomerantz.com

"Agreed then, Henderson - I won't network you if you don't network me."

www.SuziPomerantz.com

Nine Mindsets of Networking

The Nine Mindsets of Networking are the core philosophical underpinnings of success in any form of networking; real life or in any social media platform.

1. Fun and Ease. It is a game, it is fun if you stay open to it. Start with who you know, find out who they know. What feels easy to you? What gives you energy?

2. Become a connection-seeker ... if you are not already, make yourself driven to find connections. Connect people to each other, connect people to information, connect people into your life ... include them and they will include you.

3. It is about partnering: look for mutual benefit, ways to serve. Keep yourself operating from and inside of a spirit of partnership, collaboration and helpfulness.

4. Ideally, you'd have no agenda. If you do have any, however, keep your agendas clear and communicated up front. Include people in what you are up to...share, communicate. Be honest and check assumptions. Speak of that which is important to you. Find out what matters to them.

5. Curiosity about what's possible: show genuine interest in others. Inquire as to what is important to others. Be more interested than interesting. «You can make more friends in two months by becoming interested in other people than you can in two years by trying to get other people interested in you.» -- Dale Carnegie

6. Six degrees of separation: everyone is on the squad -- no benchwarmers or spectators. Strengthen the strands of your web constantly. Nothing is a wasted interaction. Every moment is an opportunity for relatedness, every relatedness moment is a building block for your network. Every strand in your web adds strength to the fibers of your network and eventually you will find it working for you. Nowadays, with social media, we are no longer six degrees away from anyone we'd want to meet...we are at most two degrees of separation away! Imagine the opportunities!

7. Climate and environment of comfort and ease. Safety/normalization/creating a comfortable atmosphere (there are three things all people want: to be respected, to be acknowledged, to be taken care of/ well-served). Seek first to understand other people (like Stephen R. Covey says) and be trustworthy.

www.SuziPomerantz.com

8. Giver's gain...people want to help you, focus on helping them and it will come back to you. Like Bob Burg says, be a «go-giver»!

9. Action. Networking is ongoing, not at events only. Never underestimate the power of informational interviews! Make calls, set up meetings, follow-up with everyone. Continual follow up and good manners will take you far.

Distinguishing Between Networking, Marketing, and Sales

People often misuse the term Marketing to be an all-encompassing concept to mean everything from press, exposure, pricing, referrals, networking and branding to sales, business development, rainmaking, and getting new clients. Marketing is often broadly used to refer to the act of getting your message/product/service to market as well as to define the materials and design of your image. I'd like to try to un-co-mingle the three main concepts for you. Once you have a clear understanding of the distinctions between networking, marketing, and sales, you will be able to manage your time so that you are leveraging each piece of this critical trinity to get to the sweet spot where deals are sealed!

In a nutshell, Networking is about Relation, Marketing is about Preparation, and Sales is about Implementation. What does that mean? Figure 1.1 will give you specifics about each one, but basically Networking is the relational aspect of your business. It is connecting with others for the purpose of sharing resources, information, leads, referrals, ideas, etc. Cultivating a working network of relationships is crucial to your business development system, but in and of itself will not be the way you build or expand your client base. Marketing is how you will prepare yourself to take your unique identity package, your irresistible offer, and your message to market. This involves a lot of strategy, design work, writing, and outreach, but those things alone will not get you the clients you want. Sales activities are about implementing your business development strategies. Simply put, Sales involves making appointments, seeking to be of service, making fabulous and bold offers, and asking for the business. Your goal is to master the integration of where preparation and relation meet implementation.

Relation + Preparation + Implementation = CLIENTS

Or, stated another way,

Networking + Marketing + Sales = \$\$\$\$

Many savvy and successful businessfolk will tell you that it is not a one to one ratio, and that it is most important to spend the bulk of your time in networking or relational activities. If you think of systems, you have to put a lot into the system up front to yield the desired output. Networking and marketing activities are the precursors to sales activities, all of which are necessary input. It isn't magic. Your networking and marketing activities do not always just naturally lead to a hot prospect and then you turn on the sales juice or begin the sales process. Although that will happen on occasion, wouldn't you rather be in the driver's seat than waiting for your networking and marketing efforts to pay off? There's no need to wait for someone to ask you to dance…you get to take the lead and thereby control your time, your efforts, your results, your business. Taking action in your sales process from the start will dramatically reduce the time-to-close even while you are building your network and creating your marketing materials and strategies.

The Figure 1.1 provides more detail about the distinctions between the three keys to success. If you take only one thing away from this book, my core message is that you need to be taking action in ALL THREE DOMAINS simultaneously to grow your business.

Figure 1.1 Distinguishing Networking, Marketing, and Sales

NETWORKING	MARKETING	SALES
Relation	**Preparation**	**Implementation**
Pipeline building	Positioning yourself	Contracting
Connection-seeking with genuine interest in others	Market research – studying the market, knowing what the market will yield, understanding market trends and influences, shopping the market for your competitors	Understanding sales cycle and process
Meeting people	Strategy, conceptual approaches	Knowing your hit rates and numbers
Talking to people and getting to know them better	Planning activities for acquisition, retention, or reacquisition of buyers	Tracking progress
Getting out there and creating relationships of all kinds	Alone in your office, in front of your computer	Making calls
Asking to meet other people – asking for introductions or at least contact information and permission to use you as a contact reference	Providing information about who you are and what you do: shameless self-promotion!	Setting up appointments with the express agenda of finding out about the current issues a prospect is facing

Figure 1.1 Distinguishing Networking, Marketing, and Sales continued...

Networking	Marketing	Sales
Follow up	Showing people what you do, perhaps including pro bono work	Client meetings to tell people what you do
Manners, etiquette, social graces	Creating text, writing letters, researching clients and prospects	Proposals
Introducing people to each other with an eye to expanding others' networks	Writing and publishing articles, columns, books	Follow-up
Activities that yield human connection and interaction, not necessarily related to business	Speaking engagements, teaching opportunities	Moving people through your pipeline
Nine Mindsets of Networking	PR and Media, Advertising	Activities that directly yield clients, contracts, business dollars
Finding out what people do, where they do it, why they do it and what they want to do	Website or brochure building, fine-tuning, management	Action Selling System
	Image and collateral things: logo, letterhead, business cards, etc.	

Figure 1.1 Distinguishing Networking, Marketing, and Sales continued...

Networking	Marketing	Sales
	Activities that yield informative materials (documents, speeches, advertising, promotional materials, stuff to hand out or direct people to)	
	Branding (sustainable, consistent, recognizable, uniqueness)	

Yeah, But What About Social Media?

Glad you asked!

Strategies for success with online networking:

- Be yourself
- Have a clear and consistent strategy and purpose that's aligned with your passions and interests
- Be a go-giver (as opposed to a go-getter)
- Be professional: always consider your brand
- Choose a few that you can engage with, as all the social media platforms are different and offer you different reach. Which ones best align with your overall strategy and brand?
- Use time-saving third-party apps to be more efficient (socialoomph.com, twitterfeed.com, ping.fm, tweetdeck.com or seesmic.com, dossy.org/twitter/karma, tinyurl.com or tr.im to shorten your urls)
- Make all your social networking platforms, including your blog, all work together in strategic concert.

You're probably already on Linked In, but are you using it as effectively as possible?

1. Make your profile work for you. Indicate on your profile whom you are looking to meet, what introductions would be most helpful to you, or how connections on Linked In can best connect with you. Indicate in your profile if you are an open networker, and if you are on Twitter or Facebook, so that you can get some cross-pollination going!

2. There's a small update field on Linked In, not unlike those on Twitter and Facebook. Use it! Share links there, let people know what you're working on, or what type of folks you're looking to meet. Make requests!

3. Find the Question and Answer sections of Linked In. Beware of posting a question, you will get many responses and common etiquette indicates that you should take the time to respond and thank each responder. To save time, respond to questions others have posted, particularly when they are asking about your subject matter expertise.

4. Join Groups. There are a ton of groups about every industry or topic of interest you can imagine. Join many! That allows you to follow (and post to) the discussion topics in each group, which is a great way to connect with like-minded folks and expand your network.

facebook

There are two ways to be on Facebook. You can set up a profile page where people can «friend» you. Or, you can set up a page for your business, called a Fan Page, where people do not become your friend, they become a fan. Or, you can have both.

1. Do customize your Facebook profile page with pictures (keep it professional!), videos, and links.

2. Comment on the «wall» of people you know who are well-connected and influential. Why? Because all their «friends» will see your post. If you include a link, you'll drive traffic to that link, especially if you are commenting on the wall of someone who has reached the 5,000 friend limit.

3. There's an app you can use called Static FBML, which allows you to basically put html code on your Facebook page. This is great for carrying your brand over to your page as well as for putting sign up or opt-in boxes on Facebook.

4. Become a fan of people, products, and organizations you trust or admire. It will help Facebook to suggest more people for you to friend so you can grow your network. All you do is click a button, and it allows them to communicate with you on another level

inside Facebook. You can become a fan of my page here, if you wish: http://tinyurl.com/spfacebookfanpage

Naymz

Naymz is cool and different because it has a reputation scorecard. You earn reputation points by having people you know attest to your reputability and trustworthiness. They can even write a testimonial or endorsement for you as well, and you for them. This is an interesting twist, because you get to see and connect with people based on how their contact rate their reputation.

Twitter is by far my favorite of the tools, because it is the fastest, creates the most results in the shortest amount of time, and is most aligned with real-world networking mindsets.

1. On Twitter, be sure to create your screen background in a way that allows you to share with people at a glance what you do and how to connect with you beyond Twitter. (Joel Comm's book, TwitterPower does a great job of explaining how to do this.)

2. Relationships on Twitter are not required to be reciprocal, so follow a LOT of people. Follow anyone who interests you, find out who they are following, and follow anyone of interest in their list.

3. The only way to make money on Twitter is NOT TO SELL. Twitter is like a huge party, and you'd never walk into a party and say, "hi, check out what I'm selling", right? Don't do it on Twitter, either. Create conversations, get to know people, see what others are saying before you jump in.

4. Automate to save time! For instance, I use twiterfeed.com to have my blog hook up to Twitter, so that anytime I post a blog post, it automatically shows up on Twitter with a link to my site. Whenever anyone follows me, I automatically follow them back using socialoomph.com (formerly tweetlater.com). Then I can follow up later with a personal direct message to connect when I have time, but this way everyone gets an immediate response.

Now, here's the key to all of this: You must integrate so that they all work together! I have my Twitter hooked up to Facebook and Linked In so that whenever I (or my blog through twitterfeed) post to Twitter, it automatically also shows up in the update of the other two platforms. Or, when I want to post something everywhere at once, I use ping.fm to save time and broadcast a quote or link to all my social networks at once.

Ta da! Maximum outreach with minimal effort.

Social Media and You: 3 Tips for Internet Networking Etiquette

Ah, the changing landscape of networking…I wanted to connect with you about the social media networking vehicles like LinkedIn, Plaxo, Naymz and Facebook to name just a few. It's amazing how many of these have popped onto the scene and it seems everyone is racing to create a professional profile and build a professional network using the latest technology. I, too, have fallen prey to the novelty of it all, and I've been finding the etiquette and ethics of what is and is not appropriate in each one of these tools to vary. So, how are we to navigate these waters?

Recently, I posted a question on Linked In to my network about the appropriateness of using LinkedIn to promote a new product I wanted to announce, as well as a new product of a colleague that I wanted to announce. Interestingly enough, the responses I got back were all across the map! Apparently nobody knows the answer to what is appropriate and/or ethical with regards to using these networks for online marketing, but everybody had a personal preference or opinion about what it should be or not be.

So, if you've read *Seal the Deal*, you know I'm an advocate of integrating your marketing, networking and sales activities, and doesn't it seem like these new social media formats are the perfect vehicle for just that? Well, beware! Right now the internet world of social networking is a wild, wild west so exercise caution in the following ways:

1.   **Beware of brand impact.** Do not create for yourself an accidental brand by posting photos of you engaged in various stages of debauchery on your Facebook page and then being shocked when your prospective employer (or current employer) or prospective or current clients use that data in their decision-making. Your credibility is as important on the internet as it is when you're wearing a suit and trying to be professional! For those of you in leadership roles, you want to be sure that your employees are not finding compromising photos of you on Facebook…even if you didn't post them, how can you be sure what your old college chums are posting?

2.   **Beware of the name-gamers.** There are a lot of folks who are just out to get as many names as they can in their networks, but these are the equivalent of empty calories. Do not sign up for any of those services or scams about getting thousands of followers. Getting names on the list is not networking. Getting names of real people with whom you have some common interest or connection is really the point of it all.

3.   **Beware of strangers.** Your online networks, like your real-life network, should be filled with people you know, trust, have an actual relationship with or experience with, and with whom you have some genuine human connection.

Remember the Nine Mindsets of Networking! Social networking works best when you follow the same principles of regular, real-life networking. Social networking online is no substitute for the actual activity of real-life networking. It can complement your actual networking activities, but should not replace them! You can learn more about the Nine Mindsets of Networking if you purchase the **Rainmaking Made Easy** audio success kit, now availablea at www.RainmakingMadeEasy.com anytime.

What's Better for Coaches? Twitter, LinkedIn, or Facebook?

Well, I use all three, amongst many other lesser known social media like Naymz and Ecademy. I like each one for different reasons. I'll share with you what I see the differences to be and how I use each one differently. Keep in mind, I'm just an executive coach figuring this stuff out as I go along…I'm no technogeek social media guru! Here goes:

Twitter:

This is streaming conversation tool that allows you to engage in multiple conversations in real time, anytime. This can be good and bad. I always turn it off during coaching

www.SuziPomerantz.com

calls, otherwise I'd be distracted! For networking and real-time information-sharing, Twitter can't be beat. It's like an ongoing party and you can network your heart out day or night from the comfort of your own computer or cell phone. Great people, great community, and one of my twitterbuddies recently said she thinks of Twitter as her always-available personal Mastermind Group. I love that!

Mindset: Create connections and seek to help and add value in micro-conversations. Relationships aren't necessarily reciprocal on Twitter. Be a go-giver!

Strategy: Initially, follow tons of people who interest you...either other coaches, authors, leadership experts, leaders of companies, or even political or celebrity figures and engage in conversations on Twitter with these folks. That way, all their followers will see your stream of conversation and can choose to follow you if the topics interest them.

Pitfall to avoid: Don't get on Twitter to just sell your services or promote your products.

LinkedIn:

This is the first social networking vehicle I ever engaged in, but I use it the least of the three mentioned here. It's a great place to collect professional contacts, to demonstrate your knowledge or subject matter expertise in the answers, and to build community of similar interests using the questions feature. The best part of LinkedIn is the groups. There are a lot of great coaching groups on there that I learn a lot from and enjoy connecting there with colleagues. Most folks outside of coaching use LinkedIn for recruiting and job-seeking, but there are still applications for us coaches.

Mindset: Keep it professional, use your profile for marketing and branding, and engage in answers to questions that demonstrate your value-add.

Strategy: Join lots of groups that interest you and engage in discussions in those groups. Become an open-networker and accept every invitation to link to you!

Pitfall to avoid: Don't invite people to link to you who do not know you well, because if a few people click that they don't know you in response to your invitation, LinkedIn will block you from inviting more people.

Facebook:

I love this one for the versatility of it. Unlike Twitter, relationships on Facebook must be approved and two-ways. You invite people to be your friend and they invite you to be their friend. You can post blog posts, videos, you can share videos and blogs that are not even yours, you can find long-lost friends and schoolmates, you can share pictures.

As a coach, it is great for keeping up with other coaches, past clients, and industry leaders. This is a great marketing vehicle for promoting your coaching activity.

Mindset: be careful what you post, not only on your Facebook pages, but comments you might write on other people's walls. Think branding, and be judicious about how much personal stuff to put out there.

Strategy: Engage in conversations (wall-to-wall) posts with industry leaders, because those are visible to everyone in your friend list as well as theirs. Keep all your photos professional and more on the business side than the family side. Set up a Facebook page for your business as well as yourself. If you have a book, set up a facebook page for your book and get "fans".

Pitfall to avoid: Facebook apps that do not align with your passion or professional image. No need to accept every invitation for an app, event or group that comes your way.

www.SuziPomerantz.com

© Mike Baldwin / Cornered

"It's too easy to lose a business card.
A rubber stamp, you'll remember."

Practice Tips: Networking, Marketing, and Sales

It is easy to spend lots of time on marketing activities, but those alone don't get you contracts.

Time spent on networking and marketing activities is time not spent on sales activities. The ideal would be a 3 to 1 ratio: three units of time spent on networking for every one unit of time spent on marketing and three units of time spent on sales for every one unit of time spent on networking.

The trick with networking is to keep active about following up with folks, even if they are not prospective clients and are not in your sales pipeline. Just keep looking for ways to help people you interact with and keep looking for more people to meet.

The trick with sales is it's all about the numbers and tracking those numbers: how many sales activities are you doing each day? How many prospective clients are in your pipeline at any given moment? How many times are you following up with folks in your pipeline?

Sales is a process, and it takes time to move through that process.

If you are resisting sales (afraid of rejection, not wanting to bug people, feeling uncomfortable), the tendency is to focus on marketing activities and congratulate yourself for getting all your ducks in a row…that's not sales. Don't trick yourself into thinking time spent on marketing activities is directly forwarding your sales. Spend more time instead on networking so that you can collect people without feeling like you are asking for anything. Then look to see how you can link sales to your core values.

Marketing activities are easier for most of people in that you can see accomplishment more quickly. You write a document, you end up with a document. Sales activities can be ongoing for weeks, months, even years before you see a tangible result.

Networking is not just for extroverts! Marianne Williamson, in *Return to Love*, wrote these words of encouragement:

"Our deepest fear is not that we are inadequate. Our deepest fear is that we are powerful beyond measure. It is our light not our darkness that most frightens us. We ask ourselves, "Who am I to be brilliant, gorgeous, talented and fabulous." Actually,

who are you NOT to be? Your playing small doesn't serve the world. There is nothing enlightened about shrinking so that others won't feel insecure around you. We are born to manifest the glory that is within us. It is in everyone. And as we let our own light shine, we unconsciously give others permission to do the same. As we are liberated from our own fear, our presence automatically liberates others."[1]

Teleclass Conversation about Ongoing Networking

---

[1] Marianne Williamson, A Return to Love: Reflections on the Principles of A Course in Miracles. (New York: Harper Collins, 1992). Chapter 7, Section 3.

[**Suzi**] On one of the early calls, we talked about the distinction between networking, marketing, and sales. So now we're going to focus on the piece of the triangle about networking, which is really about seeking connections. It's not about closing the sale, or having the meetings, and it's not about the precursor to that, which is all the image building stuff and the writing and the presentations and the stuff like that -- that's marketing. What we're going to talk about now is the ongoing activity of networking and the networking mindsets.

What are the mindsets that are helpful in seeking as many network connections as you can, building your network to a place where it can work for you, where it can help support your marketing efforts and your sales efforts? To start out I'd like to go and have each of you say what networking is for you. Then we'll get into the Nine Mindsets.

[Jeremy] For me, networking is the big schmooze . . . where in a very nice and friendly way you're like Velcro with the people you run across in work and your seminars and stuff. You follow up with them and you keep some kind of a relationship going.

[Deb] I'm the conference queen . . . And networking I think is probably my strength. Being the eternal extrovert, I can just about talk to anybody, anywhere. I can do great at the initial meeting, and what I'd like to talk about is how you keep it going.

[**Suzi**] How to have it work for you?

[Deb] Right. Because I've got tons of contacts and stuff like that, and it's just where do you put your energy and how do you make it work for you?

[**Suzi**] Yes, it does take a lot of energy and you can't keep up with everybody.

[Jeremy] So, that's sort of the next question right?

[Deb] Yeah. And one other question would be how do you target who you network with?

[**Suzi**] So we'll deal with how you target them and how you keep up with it and how to be more strategic about it. Okay, who's next?

[John] It's your strength, Deb, but it's my weakness -- making the initial contacts and schmoozing. I'm the most internal of internals, and so initiating a relationship, that type of stuff, is really tough for me.

[Bill] I'm on the borderline between introvert and extrovert. Networking for me is like putting on a suit, sort of talking the talk and becoming that. I kind discover who I am in that world when I do it. I gain confidence when I network. The closer I get to the thing, the more confident I am. So networking is a good thing for me. But I've got a lot of cards I collected at the end of the year when I did my first networking thing and, I tell you, you can waste an awful lot of time networking. I feel like I need to walk around with a billboard sign when I network: 'call me if and only if . . . . ' I don't have time to follow up with all them.

[Jeremy] And you're running into people who are also sellers, but you need to find buyers.

[Bill] Yeah, too many coaches who want to have lunch with me. It's like who needs this?

[Suzi] Well, you know what? That brings up an opportunity. Is there something you can sell to the coach?

[Bill] No, I don't want to do that. I don't think they have any money.

[Suzi] Oh, how funny. That's great. Observe your assumption. There are actually quite a few coaches who have multi-million dollar operations. Okay, did we get everybody?

[Len] Well, I pretty much think networking is like advertising myself to other people, and I would hope these people are the buyers. Also they tell me what their needs are, amongst the buyers. So that's part of networking.

[Suzi] I can see how if you equate networking with advertising yourself you'd only consider doing it with prospective buyers. I hope to expand your thinking here a bit.

Networking Mindsets

[Suzi] I'm going to share with you my Nine Mindsets of Networking. The idea with these Nine Mindsets is that they are to be used in conjunction with each other. I mean it's good to have one or more of them working for you, but using all 9 of them together is the real secret to success in networking. Networking gives you access to so many other opportunities, not just for direct dollars and sales, but for all kinds of connections throughout life.

The first mindset of networking is to think of it as a game. Networking is fun if you stay open to it as a game. The trick is to start with the people you already know. As we went around the group, what I heard in common in what each of you said is that networking is "a thing that you go to" -- that it has to do with meeting people for the first time and being an extrovert even if you are an introvert, it has to do with collecting business cards. Something else you said is that it requires a lot of follow up, and it's very time-consuming. If you think of it as a game, and if you stay open to the fun of it as a game, and if you start with the people you already know, it's a lot more fun. It's not so much this task that you have to manage, with the time and the cards and making yourself an extrovert if you're not, and on and on. Networking is not about being outgoing if you aren't, it is about a sincere curiosity and interest in other people.

Start with who you know and systematically find out who they know. It's just like referrals for sales. You're going for the warm leads. If you network, if your networking is around warm leads . . . Now you're not going for people who are specific to anything directed at your business; at this point networking is just everyone. So that's the first mind set: **Networking is fun if it involves people who you already know -- just start with who they know.**

The second mindset is: Become a connection-seeker. Now if you're not already doing this, make yourself driven to find connections. What that means is look to connect people with each other, connect people with information, connect people into your life -- include people, and ask them to include you. Most of the time you don't even have to ask, because if you're including people in your life, and if you're connecting them with information and what you're up to, they're going to start including you in things. And it snowballs from there. So the second mindset is: **Be a connection-seeker.**

The third mindset is about partnership, and that's just partnership in the general sense of the term. Look for mutual benefit, look for ways to serve the people that you're networking with -- whether you're meeting them for the first time, or whether they're warm leads, or whether they're people you already know. I've heard it called servant leadership. Ask questions like these: 'What   are things we can help each other do? What are you up to in your life? What are you interested in? What's important to you? What are you working on? What are your challenges?'

And when you're exploring and you're genuinely curious about that, you'll find all kinds of ways you can connect with them. The point here is that you **focus more on being *interested* instead of trying to be *interesting*.** You might be able to find leads for babysitters, I think I shared that example with you before. You know, you might say, 'I just read an article that speaks exactly to your point, I'll fax it over to you'. There's so many ways that you can connect with people and look for mutual benefit, look for ways to serve them.

[Jeremy] That's what I mean by the big schmooze . . . You're just spreading out your influence. **There are layers upon layers of ways that you serve people in your network, and you just look of connect to them.** And it might not have anything to do with what your initial outcome will be or what you hope. It might just be on a very basic level.

[Suzi] Exactly, and that goes back to mindset #2, being a connection-seeker, because if you're genuinely focused on that, and if your only agenda is to seek connections, then you're going to find usefulness in every person you interact with. And you're looking to find ways to be useful to them. So it's not just about sales. With sales you are strategically targeting people in your network for the purpose of selling your services. And the purpose of those conversations is to get meetings, and the purpose of those meetings is to get more meetings, etc. There's a focus to it, there's a strategy to it, it's purposeful. You are focused on those who would be buyers of your services with sales, but not with networking.

Networking to me is very expansive. With networking, you're meeting people in your life, you're meeting the people in their life, you're finding out where the connections are, you're just exploring possibilities. There's no "should" or "have to" about it -- it's just about a genuine curiosity about what's there. It's like going on a scavenger hunt, looking for something that might be out there. Assuming there's something there, and looking for it, and keep looking. Sometimes you keep looking and you find there's nothing there, and then you just go your separate ways. But most of the time if you're looking hard enough you'll find something to connect with people about.

*The fourth mindset is about **keeping your agendas clear and communicated** up front*. Networking gets hard when people go to networking events with the intention of selling something. Sometimes I find people are there to give out their card or collect cards, or because they want to talk about their particular service that they want you to buy. That's not networking, that's selling. Networking is where you're just there to make connections. You're in it to meet this person, to explore who this person is and what are the ways that you two can play together -- and if you do have an ulterior agenda you want to communicate it up front. You want to be honest, and you want to check your assumptions -- that's part of keeping the agenda clear and communicated up front. If you have an assumption that the two of you are having a conversation simply to explore what's possible in having met each other or getting to know each other further, check that out -- I wouldn't assume anything.

The fifth mindset is a **curiosity about what's possible and a genuine interest in others** all the time. And again that ties back into being the connection-seeker. Be more interested than interesting.

The sixth mindset is based on the six-degrees-of-separation concept -- are you familiar with that one? The concept is that we are all, everybody in the world, separated by only six other people between us -- six degrees of separation. So, for example, even though I met each of you for the first time over the phone when we began this class, if we sat down one at a time and explored everybody that we know, chances are we are six people or less away from each other. In other words, I know somebody who knows somebody who knows somebody who knows you -- five somebodies in between us, rendering us six people apart from each other.

The other way that this concept works is when there's somebody that you'd like to get to know. Let's say you wanted to get to know Bill Clinton. The odds are, there are only six other people between you and Bill Clinton. There's a chain of people who know each other that's only 6 people deep, between you and anybody you want to get to know.

In that mindset, the application to networking is that everyone is on the squad -- there are no benchwarmers or spectators in this sport. So nothing is a wasted interaction . . . **There is no wasted time in networking because everyone is connected, and if they're not connected to someone you want to know, they *are* someone you want to know.** And part of getting to know all the different people that you could possibly want to know in your life is you're constantly strengthening the strands of your web, if you think of networking as a big spider web. Actually it's more like a net -- you are in a net of people all connected by different strands. And let's say there are people in your life you haven't talked to, or let's say you had great connections at conferences you went to with people whose business cards you kept but never followed up with. Those strands are very weak and thin right now, and the way to strengthen them is by having the conversations and following up and getting to know those people more.

So, with the mindset of six degrees of separation and everyone being on the squad, every moment is an opportunity for relatedness. And every opportunity for relatedness is a building block for your network. So every strand in your web, every strand in your net, adds strength to the fibers of your network. And if you're just focusing on strengthening all those strands, eventually you're going to find that it all starts working for you.

www.SuziPomerantz.com

[Jeremy] Here's one way it works: when you're going for leads, whether it's a networking lead or a sales lead, you don't go away empty handed, you leave with another name.

[Suzi] Right. For me that's more specific to sales, because there's a 'should-do' implied in that, so it's more strategic . . .   But the way I think about networking, it's an ongoing thing, it's all the time. It's not something that you do when you think about it. Sales activities are something I have to remember to do, and something I have to schedule to do, and something I have to keep track of in terms of where I am in the process. And networking is not. Networking is just ongoing, all the time. I'm not just strategically seeking connections or leads related to business, I'm just seeking connections in general with everyone, everywhere, all the time.

[John] Even if you don't exchange business cards?

[Suzi] Exactly. Networking is not about the business cards. Business cards are about marketing. Networking is about these Nine Mindsets working together.

   Okay, mindset #7 is wanting to create a comfortable atmosphere for the people that you're talking with. It's about keeping in mind, as you're building relationships, that there are three things that people want. **People want to be loved. People want to be acknowledged. And people want to be taken care of.**[2] Being taken care of can mean being attended to physically, emotionally, spiritually, mentally, or simply being heard or being understood. Part of being taken care of is being well-served. In business this translates into providing excellent customer service, or exceeding expectations. But, in general, I have yet to find people who would argue with me that they don't want those three things. They want to be respected or loved, they want to be acknowledged, and they want to be taken care of. So in networking, as you're connecting with people, look for ways to do those things.

   Mindset #8 is the concept of giver's gain. The idea behind giver's gain is that if you focus on what you can provide for others, you're going to get some benefit out of that. **Rather than looking for what others can do for you, focus on what you have to offer them.** It's like President Kennedy's "Ask not what your country can do for you but what you can do for your country" -- it's that concept. If you're the giver you're going to gain. Because generally people want to help you, so if you're focusing on helping them, it will come back to you. The last mindset is the notion that networking is ongoing, all the time -- it's not just at networking events, it's not just at conferences, it's

---

[2] Alice Miller, who wrote The Drama of the Gifted Child, rev. ed. (New York: Basic Books, 1996) says that all people want to be respected, understood, and taken seriously.

not when you put on your suit, it's not just when you make sure you have all your business cards with you and go forth with the intention. **Networking requires constant action.**

Networking Vehicle: Informational Interviews

One of the things that I found really helpful in getting started in networking is the informational interview. That's a really powerful tool for meeting people and getting connected with who's in their life. For example, as you know, I was a schoolteacher before I became a coach and business owner. When I left teaching I knew there was some other thing out there I wanted to do, I just didn't know what it was. So when I set forth, I didn't have a business network -- I had been a teacher, and my network was my students and the other teachers in the school. So I set out to meet people in business. And I started with the people I knew through family and friends. I said, 'Who do you know who's in business? I don't care what business, I want to go meet with them and do an informational interview and find out who they are and what they do and what skills it requires and whether or not it's something that a teacher could transfer skills into doing'.

I spent 6 months conducting about 150 informational interviews. Now, I didn't start with 150 people, I started with 3. But what happened was, from each person I did the informational interview with, I asked for names of who else they knew that I could talk to -- who might be an interesting next step in my journey of exploring what's possible out there in terms of new careers? And that's how I met so many people and started my business as a coach -- it was through people I found through the informational interviews. I ended up meeting a woman who connected me up with the president of her company, which happened to be a coaching and development company, and they were looking at the time to bring on new associates. They had a stringent selection process, then they provided intensive training and mentoring and that's what got me started. So never underestimate the power of informational interviews.

Networking is the precursor to sales activities because in order to follow up and to keep strengthening the strands of your web, you've got to make phone calls, you've got to set up meetings, and you've got to follow up. And following up has to be ongoing. So it's not only getting out there and continually meeting new people and continually strengthening the strands of the web of people who are already in your network. It's also following up, following up, following up.

[Jeremy] And it's interesting because what we're looking to do here when we're networking is we're looking to be selfless, and giver's gain, and that's very real. On the other hand there's a time when people are going to turn to us -- after we've been very generous, connecting them to others, providing them information, giving them names, and faxing and e-mailing and all like that -- and they're going to say, 'Oh, and what do you do, who are you?' And we have to be ready to not be self-effacing at that point. We have to be ready to turn on our little commercial and tell what we've been doing, and plugging it into what they've been doing.

[Suzi] That's exactly right. And that is when networking transfers into the sales process -- at that very moment, when they express that interest in what you're up to. You have to listen for it. Because there comes a time when they're going to come to you and want to know what you do and where you do it. And this is why, in this telecourse, we didn't start with networking, which is somewhat the logical place to begin. We started with our 30-second commercial; networking is down here at class #8.

The idea is that networking is a doorway into the sales process. It's a great place to continually be keeping your pipelines fresh, and keep new things coming into the pipeline. And to answer Deb's earlier question about how you strategically target the people that you want to be networking with, my answer to that is don't. Let that go. My answer to that is network with everybody, and then when you're in the sales process be strategic about who you target in the sales process.

In networking, you want to throw open the doors, let everybody into the game. It's a big old party, it's a big game, everybody's in it. If you have that mindset about networking, you get to meet really interesting people on airplanes, and walking the dog, getting your hair cut, waiting in lines -- and you find all kinds of interesting things out about people. And it becomes like a game. And you know what else? If you keep it in your mindset as a game, you don't have to follow up on *everything*. So now, if you don't want to be strategic with who you've met in your networking, and put them into your sales process for follow up, then okay . . . yeah, I know we've said you've got to follow up, follow up, follow up with everyone. But to me networking takes all of the shoulds out of it. There are no laws about who you should network with. Network with everybody, see what comes of it. See who they know. Any reactions, comments, questions?

[Bill] A few more words about the informational interview. What is that exactly?

[Suzi] An informational interview is where you set up a meeting with someone to gather information about them, either about what they do or what their company does -- it's not a sales meeting at all. It's personal, you're looking for information that will help you figure out what's next for you. So these types of meetings are very non-threatening for the other person, because you're clearly not coming to sell them anything; you are coming to pick their brains. It's flattering for people. It's kind of like you're asking for a small nugget of mentorship, mentoring in a small dose.

So you set up the informational interview for half an hour with somebody, or you set up lunch with somebody. I actually tried not to set them up around meals, because I didn't want to have any awkward moments … At the time I was trying to live off my savings, so I didn't want to spend any unnecessary money and I didn't want anyone else to feel pressure to pick up the tab. So I would set up these half-hour meetings. I would go to someone's office and I'd say, 'Tell me about what you do, how did you get into what you do? What skills does someone have to have to be successful doing what you do? What do you like about it? What do you not like about it? What would you do differently if you had to do it over again?' And what I started learning were all the jobs that I didn't want to do after I left teaching. That's what was helpful for me, but you can design informational interviews around anything that you want to find out.

Also, there were two questions that I asked every single person in the informational interview: 'Who else do you recommend that I conduct this interview with, who else would be good to talk to?' and 'What do you recommend that I read?' And I followed up on just about all of the people, and some of the books that were suggested to me.

[Jeremy] So you *did* get another name . . .

[Suzi] At that point it wasn't sales, it was survival. I had to ask the person in front of me where else to find people. It's amazing, how people really want to help you. You call up and you ask for an informational interview, and they're happy to help.

[Jeremy] Well, people like other people who are vulnerable. Which speaks to an interesting networking and sales and interpersonal dynamic. It's one thing to come across as authoritative and know your stuff, but it's also great if you can provide a balance –– that there are areas that you'd like to get help in. People like that vulnerability.

[Suzi] I think that's right. So, does this approach to networking sound far-fetched for you, or does this sound like something you could integrate into what you're already doing? If not, where are the obstacles for you?

[Deb] It's pretty much a lot of what I've been doing, and I think I need to take it to the next step, because I'm very much a connector and putting people together and networking and all that stuff. So now I need to go to the next stage and really keep in touch with some of these people, and following through with some of the connections. I have a question, though. You mentioned a word, before the Nine Mindsets . . . you said 'strategic'. Can you clarify what you meant?

[Suzi] That's more in the sales process. When you're in the sales process, you want to identify all the people in your network. And by network I mean all of the people you know. Everybody, even your three-year-old's best friend. There are people that you know who know other people. So look in your network and find out who, of the universe of people in your network, are strategic choices for you to plug into your sales process for business. In other words, if you had to focus your attention on just a handful of people in that network to pursue for a possible business development, who would those people be? That becomes your target list, and it isn't a list of everyone in the world; you strategically select it for the purposes of selling your services.

And then part of doing that is figuring out how you're going to access them. It may make sense to look at how you know those people. Let's say there's someone in your network that you know through your next-door neighbor. So maybe the way you're going to access that person is to have your next-door neighbor help you connect up with that person. It all depends on the relationship . . .

And sometimes it's helpful to trace back how you know people, to keep the connection, the strands of the web, clear in your mind. Who connected you to whom? How did you met this or that person, and trace the connections to see how many degrees of separation back they go. When I started doing this I could trace my very first client back through six people. I could trace all the way back to the person who started the ball rolling, the one person that I already knew who said, 'you should talk to this person'. And then I met that person and they said, 'Oh, you should talk to this person'. It's fun sometimes to do that, to trace it back and see how it works -- and to see how long and strong some of your connections really are.

[Jeremy] Also, something else I think that we can all identify in ourselves about networking is a continual availability, an openness. To be able to be open to new possibilities of connecting to other people, and thinking we don't have to judge them, they don't have to judge us. In Myers-Briggs terms, I think networking is the ultimate key activity. You don't have closure. It's the opposite of project management. You're not managing any projects here, it's just keeping things open. Playfulness generates connections from others and an interest from others in playing. In the course of that expansiveness, you find out if there are possibilities for other forms of relating, ideally in terms of business.

[**Suzi**] There are so many things that we have to do, that are 'should-dos'. And for me the sales process has a lot of 'should-dos' in it, but networking is just a place to sort of let your hair down and be fun and see what's possible. That's a lot of what attracts me to coaching; it is the exploration or commitment to what's possible and for me networking is just a natural place to express that.

[Jeremy] Suzi, do you have a specific networking strategy for being in conferences or trainings, aside from giving out your business card and taking business cards?

[**Suzi**] Yes, I would forget about the business card game and design for yourself a strategy or a goal for what you want to accomplish networking-wise, during that time. So that you're not just sitting there listening for the content, but you also have a strategy: who you want to meet and what you want to find out about who you meet. What is your goal for the meeting or conference? What do you want to accomplish? Who are the kinds of people that are going to be there, and **how can you be useful to them** and how can they be useful to you, and how many do you want to meet? It's different for me with each meeting I go to. Sometimes I'm at a conference and I'm looking to just meet as many new people as I can. And sometimes my strategy is more specific, and I know there's going to be one or two people that I know are going to be there that I want to meet, so I'm going to seek those people out. Or maybe there are people that I've talked to or come in contact with that I've never met in person. And so my strategy is to put faces with names and deepen my relationships with people that I have at least a superficial contact with. So that's what I'd say just in a nutshell, just **have a goal or a strategy for every networking interaction**. The key at any networking event, (i.e., any event where there are people), is to meet as many new people as you can through the people that are there that you already know. If you don't know anyone, introduce yourself to one person who seems to know everyone, and ask them to introduce you around.

[Deb] Okay. That's helpful because I'm still in the stage of 'what can I bring to you?' So it's helpful in forcing me to think in that way.

[**Suzi**] Just identify for yourself what you want to learn at these conferences. Not just from the speakers, but what do you want to find out from your colleagues that will be there with you?

[Jeremy] Now, sometimes the people at those conferences that are often sought-after, are very defensive, they're so used to being hit on by people who are trying to sell them, that they're really weary of any kind of interaction with somebody new. So it's important to just try to get them outside the conference, or to make an appointment to

www.SuziPomerantz.com

talk to them or be with them later on, where you're finding about what their needs are. Because they're just burnt out by sales pitches.

[Suzi] You know, there's nothing wrong with having your strategy be to seek out your colleagues. Especially if you're in a transition phase. You could have your whole strategy be to meet other coaches who are going to be there, to ask them some strategy questions about how they handle different things, or what their approach is, or what their strategies are. Because I find that folks in the coaching community are so open that it's a great time to gather information and you might get some good ideas for how you're doing things.

[Deb] Yeah, that's my goal. I think it's kind of turning it around, and seeing what kind of value do they actually bring, and how do I differ and how am I the same?

[Suzi] Keep it distinct, too. This is a networking event, not a sales event. You're not there to sell, **the purpose is not to sell anything, the purpose is really to make contacts, make connections, and develop relationships.** And there's nothing wrong either with having your strategy be, 'I'm just going to see who's drawn to me and see what comes of it.'

[Jeremy] This is a good chance to work on your 30-second commercial.

[Deb] Exactly, that's what I was thinking about. And there are going to be some people from companies there. So it is an opportunity to maybe promote. But I think I can come in the side door on that.

[Suzi] See what your comfort level is, too, I always get burned out more quickly at a conference if I'm trying to promote than if I'm just creating relationships to explore later.

[Bill] This is good news to me, because too often I walk away from networking experiences and say, 'Well, nothing's really come of that, I've collected a bunch of cards . . . and how many of these people are selling insurance?' But it's good to know that it's a much more open-ended thing, and that it's as much social and recreational as it is anything else -- and you never know what comes of these things.

[Suzi] Exactly. You could meet your next best friend in a random networking incident. You just don't know. I would say take the focus off of the cards. Take the focus off of giving your card out and collecting their cards. If you get cards from people that you know you're never going to want to keep in touch with, throw them out; there's no reason to keep them just because they gave them to you. I find people all the time who just have stacks and stacks and stacks of business cards with rubber bands around them, from every conference they've ever gone to.

[Bill] Also I feel very guilty. If someone's e-mailing me and they want to get together for lunch, and I don't want to get together with this person. Or there's someone who wants to show me space in his school business program in case I want to rent it out later. I feel guilty about not following up with these people. I e-mailed them something polite, but I need to get away from that too. The way we're talking about networking now it seems like a very loose, not necessarily responsive, thing.

[Suzi] Right. The trouble that I find a lot of people get into is that they confuse networking with sales activities. And the person who wants you to look at space for the possible future time when you might consider renting -- that's someone who has confused networking with sales. Because if that person were being strategic about contacting you for a specific sales purpose, they would have already figured out that you're not interested in pursuing that further. But because they've couched it in terms of networking, you're now left with all of this 'should' feeling around following up with them. So it gets messy . . . which is why we want to keep networking distinct from sales, which goes back to the mindset about keeping agendas communicated and clear up front.

In networking, true networking, you don't owe them anything, you don't have to go follow up, you don't have to go look at anything. If you're networking, you're exploring connections and possibilities. And for you, looking at that space is not a possibility, so you don't have to explore that. I see this most often with attorney clients that I coach. Because they don't really have any concept of sales activities as being distinct from networking. They think that if they're networking, they're selling. And they don't see the distinction, they have it completely collapsed. So part of my challenge for them is to un-collapse that. To help them see that in fact, networking is X, and sales is Y. And networking in and of itself does not get you clients, does not get you dollars. You get clients, develop business, and bring in dollars when you take your network that you've been building up continually, and you strategically target people in your network to bring them into your sales process -- which is everything we have been talking about for the last 8 classes.

[John] So, Bill, a way to get the folks off your e-mail tail is to just call it what it is, and tell them something like, 'I enjoyed meeting you, but I'm not in the market'.

[Suzi] Exactly. No harm in that. Another possibility is to go and meet with these people for lunch or to look at the space, and use that as an opportunity to explore other possible connections. And see where it leads. If you want to do that you can, and then you're taking it back into the realm of networking, and you're keeping it there, which is fine. But you don't have to let anyone else take you out of networking and into their sales process unless you want to go with them.

[John] So what you could tell them is, 'I'm not in the market, but if you'd like to have lunch anyway, I'd like to have lunch with you.'

[Suzi] Right. I'd say something like, 'we might still meet just to explore possibilities and see where we might be able to help each other.'

[Len] Right. That would be a good idea because I originally was interested in meeting with this person, and starting a small business curriculum at SUNY Purchase, which is about 10 miles from here, but then it sort of devolved into a discussion of space, and I think I fell into that too easily. This is a nice distinction.

[Suzi] Also, be assertive about how people can help you. When you go to explore this, it could be that the person who wants to sell you space picked up in conversation with you that that's something that could truly help you. You'll need to be assertive and say something like, 'Well that's really not what I'm up to right now, but I'll tell you what I am up to . . . I'm interested in meeting clients in X industry, and if you know anyone in that industry, I'd love to meet them'. Or whatever you're up to -- tell them what you're up to.

[Jeremy] Then give them your commercial.

[Suzi] Exactly. But be conscious of where you are in the networking dance, or the networking experience, and the sales process.

[Jeremy] Now another important part of networking that I just want to underline is that one of the things that we do when we network is make other people our sales representatives. Or maybe not sales representatives, more like information representatives, if you will -- they become your affiliates who can pass along referrals to you. And the more you're able to do that the more you're able to leverage your network.

[Suzi] That's right. People you meet ideally become your agents, and that's where you're going to start to see the return on the investment of time. That's where you're going to start to see your network working for you, when you've got such solid connections with people that all of a sudden they're sending you people who are clients and prospects. Because they know who you are, they know what you're up to, and they know the exact profile of people that you're interested in, and when they come across them, they'll send them to you.

www.SuziPomerantz.com

[Jeremy] And when you have those kinds of people in your network, take good care of them!

[Suzi] So go out there and explore networking in a way that is about having fun and see if you can transfer that attitude to your continued homework assignment of making calls and setting up meetings.

"Very impressive educational background...now let's discuss WHO you know."

Informational Interviews

The most powerful vehicle for networking is not exchanging cards at a business meeting designed for networking, rather it is the one-on-one genuine human connection you create when conducting informational interviews. It is based on relationship-building and introduces the keys to networking for influence and visibility.

Who's brain would you like to pick about their career path or their business model? Informational interviews allow you to request small doses of mentoring from others who are always flattered and willing to help. Continuous improvement and professional growth (not to mention business development) relies on key learnings garnered from informational interviews.

1. Design your interview questions based on your goals and the specific person you are interviewing

2. Select your interview candidates based on your goals

3. Conduct informational interviews with those who are doing what you want to do or whom you admire.

4. Remember the 80/20 rule and get them talking 80% of the time...focus on them and their perspective, not your stuff.

5. Send a thank you note

General interview questions to jump-start your brainstorming:

1.   What matters to you most?

2.   How did you get to where you currently are in your career -what was your path? Was it intentional and strategic, or organic?

3.   What lessons have you learned that you could share with me about success?

4.   What skills or best practices are required for success in what you are doing?

5.   What do you recommend I read?

6.   Whom do you recommend I talk to about this?

7.   Then, for the 20% of the conversation that is about you, it helps to have a personal platform or series of commitments and expectations you'd like the other to know about you...this may change given the particular person to whom you are speaking. How would you like to be known? Think about your brand.

www.SuziPomerantz.com

Applications of informational interviews:

1. networking in the marketplace

2. networking in-house

3. increasing visibility

4. seeking promotions

5. rapid onboarding (keys to success here, etc)

6. understanding culture

7. learning to navigate political landscape

8. building coalition

9. creating allies

10. increasing your reach and influence

11. finding out how to make things happen in a particular arena

12. finding out how you're perceived.

13. identifying patterns for career paths or success factors

14. revealing themes

15. market research

16. practice and fine-tuning a message (lobbying)

17. changing jobs

18. changing careers

19. changing industries

20. expanding leadership role

21. new team

22. new boss

23. after a merger - to learn the hotspots in the other culture

Checklist: Networking Actions

List the categories in your life in which you know people (i.e., family, church, work, neighborhood, school, past employers, business associates, friends, associations or professional groups, those who provide services to you; your dentist, etc.)

➢ Make each category a separate page and list all the people you know in each category.

➢ In each category, choose the top three people you know best as your networking starters.

➢ Set up time to talk to or be with your network starters and tell them your vision.

➢ Ask your network starters who they know that you could talk to about your vision.

➢ Seek out every person your network starters referred you to and tell them your vision.

➢ Ask each of these people whom they know that you might talk to.

➢ Continue to work your way through your own network lists.

➢ Continue to follow up and meet people from your network starters networks.

➢ Tell everyone you meet what you are up to in your business, in your life.

➢ Tell everyone a clear profile of your ideal clients.

➢ Remember the Nine Mindsets of Networking during all of these interactions!

➢ Explore collaborative, partnering and alliance-building opportunities.

➢ Identify and list at least 10 people with whom you want to do a joint venture or other collaboration and have initial conversations with them about what that might look like.

     www.SuziPomerantz.com

Getting Started or Getting Unstuck:
The Best First Step is Networking

Whether you consider yourself an introvert or an extrovert, you can find your authentic way of connecting with others. Networking is not just for the social butterflies. On average, each person has a natural network of close to 250 people. How about you?

Below are 14 networking ideas to get you going!

List the categories in your life in which you know people (i.e., family, church, work, neighborhood, school, past employers, business associates, friends, associations or professional groups, those who provide services to you; your dentist, etc.)

Make each category a separate page and list all the people you know in each category.

In each category, choose the top three people you know best as your networking starters.

Set up time to talk to or be with your network starters and tell them your vision.

Ask your network starters whom they know that you could talk to about your vision.

Seek out every person your network starters referred you to and tell them your vision.

Ask each of these people whom they know that you might talk to.

Continue to work your way through your own network lists.

Continue to follow up and meet people from your network starters' networks.

Tell everyone you meet what you are up to in your business.

Remember the Nine Mindsets of Networking during all of these interactions!

Explore partnering and alliance-building opportunities.

Identify and list at least 10 people with whom you want to do a joint venture.

Identify and list at least 10 people with whom you'd like to co-create products and service offerings.

Networking is not something you do outside of your work, or as an extra distasteful task, like taking out the trash or paying taxes…it is ongoing activity. Connect with people, meet people, talk to people, get to know what matters to people, be more interested than interesting.

Bob practices lying.

How Do Contacts Become Clients?

Leveraging Existing Relationships Into Business

How do you use the network you have without compromising your relationships with friends and family? How do you move existing networking relationships into business relationships?

Best Practices:

1. Let go of the attachment to needing business.

2. Focus on your strengths.

3. Cultivate a culturally appropriate ability for shameless self-promotion.

4. Do not seek to sell - seek to provide service.

5. Share what you love most about what you do and the difference it makes for people.

6. Share your profile of ideal clients and their struggles/problems that you can solve.

7. Let everyone know you are building your practice entirely through word of mouth and that you value their referrals.

8. Clearly articulate whom you help and what you help them to do in a way a 5-year old can understand and repeat to others.

9. Be a strategic problem-solver who matches resources in your firm with challenges and issues people in your life are facing.

10. The goal is not to turn your existing contacts into clients, but to turn THEIR existing relationships into clients.

11. Give referrals, give leads, look for ways to connect people with their ideal clients while keeping them informed about who qualifies as your ideal clients.

12. Ask for referrals, ask for business, ask for introductions, ask for leads.

13. Humbly and authentically share wins, success stories, how you helped someone and what it meant to them while giving others credit.

14. Promote others more than yourself.

www.SuziPomerantz.com

15. Build coalition with internal resources as well as industry peers.

16. Reach big and be a "yes" to all the work that can come your way, regardless of current capacity to serve that work. Trust that you'll figure it out later.

17. Make it work for you. Build relationships in a way that is comfortable and authentic to your style and personality.

18. Think strategically about how and where to build relationships.

19. Focus more on others than yourself.

20. Listen for the opportunity to shift from a networking conversation into a sales conversation.

IT'S ALL ABOUT MINDSETS

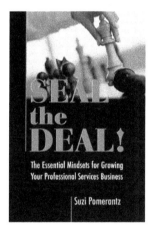

- Networking is the relational aspect of your business. It is connecting with others for the purpose of sharing resources, information, leads, referrals, ideas.
- Cultivating a working network of relationships is crucial to your business development system.
- Networking is about connecting, meeting people, collecting people.

www.innovativeleader.com

It's all about mindsets: Thoughts become things. Belief systems, attitudes, mindsets create actions which create results or lack thereof. Intervene at the level of mindsets, create alignment and congruence with commitment, and voila! RESULTS.

Aligning with your strengths and passions as motivators, style markers for your own authentic business development approach, or leadership approach, or coaching approach will serve you best, and will actually be easier and more fun, too!

Being a leader in your industry is built on a couple of key factors: 1. Networking effectively and 2. Self leadership

We've done a fair amount of explaining on the networking front. Let's look into self-leadership for a moment. Self-leadership is the key to advancing your career, your business, your success. It involves awareness at the level of leadership and can be applied in your networking activities. Just playing with the word «SELF» in self-leadership is insightful:

> Sales sophistication,
>
> Engaged enrollment,
>
> Listening/lightness,
>
> Fortitude/fulfillment

For those of us who are internal to any group or organization, the AISLE strategy to networking is a powerful approach: Align, Influence, Socialize, Lobby, Engage: *Building coalition with strategically targeted key influencers is key to managing your brand.*

Let's unpack that strategy a bit further.

Align: You want to align your networking activities and strategies, whether online or in real life, with your brand, your passions, and your personal style. In an organization, however, you want to additionally align with the objectives or mission of the organization, or you want to seek to align with individuals or groups that are likely allies for you.

Influence: When you are aligned and congruent in your beliefs, actions, and being, you can begin to influence people, factors, variables, and outcomes. In building your network and in building coalition with those who have influence already, be sure you have a clear strategy in mind for your own influence goals. Who would you like to influence and why? For what goal or purpose? How would it serve them?

Socialize: This is the act of sharing your ideas or proposed project with others, particularly others whose buy-in would support your efforts the most. For instance, my executive coaching clients create an action plan for the six months of our coaching work together, and it incorporates variables that include their goals, their organization's objectives, perhaps some feedback from others, etc. We then socialize that plan with their boss and sponsor or other stakeholders (run it by them and seek their input) to be sure we're on track and aligned.

Lobby: This is the act of sharing your ideas or proposed project with others on both sides of the equation. You want to engage vocal dissenters and folks who could potentially be opposed as well as those who are allies or prospective influencers. Why? Because you want to know what the opposition's points are. You also want to know what they want in order to have it work. If you can negotiate their buy-in, you can build influence with your network in deeper ways.

Engage: Building a network is not just an act of collecting people. You want to engage those folks and enroll them in some movement or interest, or action, or event. If you can engage your network, you can move mountains. Engagement is as simple as finding out what they are up to and what matters most to them, and seeking to help them get there. As Zig Ziglar tells us, "You can get anything you want in life if you help enough people get what they want."

Wrapping it Up

So, we've covered a lot of ground, but of course the landscape is constantly changing. If you'd like to keep up with us as new insights and tools come out, please sign up to get my blog or newsletter at www.suzipomerantz.com .

The bottom line of all this is that networking in real life and networking online are BOTH critical to anything you want to accomplish in business, leadership or coaching, and the same awareness is essential in both the real world and the online world. Of course, if you seek to be of service and take care of people, you can't lose.

So get out there and network up a storm, and let me know how it's going! Here's where you can network with me, and I'd love to hear from you:

Twitter: @suzipomerantz

Facebook Profile: http://www.facebook.com/suzipomerantz

Facebook Business Page: http://tinyurl.com/Spfacebookfanpage

Linked In: http://www.linkedin.com/in/suzipomerantz

Leading Coaches' Center: http://leadingcoachescenter.com

Naymz: http://www.naymz.com/search/suzi/pomerantz

Ecademy: http://www.ecademy.com/account.php?id=433593

TCE: http://www.thecoachexchange.com/profile/suzipomerantz

Boomer Authority: http://boomerauthority.ning.com/profile/suzipomerantz

Other: http://www.suzipomerantz.com/contact/

Appendix

Self-StudyOptions

Access more learning at a time and place of your choosing with these self-study products at various price points:

1. Tons of **free** articles are posted on my blogsite at www.suzipomerantz.com under the tab that says "Free Stuff"

2. Download more than a dozen **free** podcasts available in mp3 format to hear more concepts from Seal the Deal on your iPod or on your PC anytime, or listen online. www.innovativeleader.com/audio.htm

3. Over 25 **free** videos are available all the time at our YouTube channel: www.youtube.com/sealthedealbook

4. Access the secrets of the Rainmaking Made Easy Success Kit (10-podcast lessons, 4 hours of audio) at www.RainmakingMadeEasy.com **(LIMITED TIME: only $14.95)**

5. Buy the Seal the Deal book at www.sealthedealbook.com anytime at Amazon, Barnes and Noble, and other retailers (retails for **$24.95**)!

6. Get Going on Twitter NOW with the Twitter Tutorial program; a step by step, one-hour mp3 audio download and companion e-book for only **$47**! www.innovativeleader.com/twitterwithsuzi.htm

About Suzi

Author **Suzi Pomerantz, MT, MCC** is an <u>award-winning</u> executive coach, speaker, and facilitator with over 16 years of coaching and teaching experience working with leaders and teams in over 135 organizations internationally across Government Agencies and private sector clients, including seven companies on the Fortune 100 list. Suzi specializes in coaching at the intersection of leadership and business development, with a particular emphasis on integrating brand and social media into your strategy.

Suzi's strength lies in helping leaders and organizations find clarity within chaos. She was one of the first executive coaches to receive the Master Coach credential from the International Coach Federation over 11 years ago and is considered a thought leader in the coaching industry, serving as faculty at top coach training programs worldwide.

- Founder of the Library of Professional Coaching, a dynamic internet-based resource for coaching tools, <u>http://www.libraryofprofessionalcoaching.com</u>.
- Founder of the Leading Coaches' Center, a free online community center for top business coaches, <u>http://leadingcoachescenter.com</u>
- Founder of the Leading Coaches Clubhouse, an exclusive membership opportunity for top business coaches, <u>http://leadingcoachescenter.com/clubhouse</u>
- Founding Vice President and Executive Board Member International Consortium for Coaching in Organizations (ICCO)
- Advisory Board Member of ICCO
- Editorial Board Member of the International Journal for Coaching in Organizations (IJCO)
- Executive Board Member and past co-Chairman of the International Executive Coaching Summit
- Author, *Seal the Deal: The Essential Mindsets for Growing Your Professional Services Business* (HRD Press, 2006)
- CEO, <u>Innovative Leadership International LLC</u>

Find out more at <u>http://www.suzipomerantz.com/about-2/</u>

About ILI

Innovative Leadership International LLC (ILI) is a woman-owned executive coaching firm specializing in organizational coaching, leadership development and business development.

Innovative Leadership International LLC offers clients performance improvement expertise through powerful business coaching, management consulting, and organizational training.

The coaches and consultants of ILI specialize in leadership development, working as your partners for the success of your business.

We provide coaching, training, facilitation, and leadership development services.

ILI's Mission

Innovative Leadership International LLC develops powerful leaders and delivers outstanding value and service consistent with our commitment to organizational excellence, professionalism, and integrity.

We achieve our mission by always exceeding clients' expectations of customized training, consulting, and coaching.

We work in partnership for the success of our clients' businesses by transforming organizations through individuals.

About Seal the Deal

If you are a coach, consultant, or solopreneur who is great at what you do, but who has also been struggling with how to grow your valuable service business, we invite you to step behind the success curtain to learn the insider growth secrets that will get you booking clients and breathing easy.

Seal the Deal: The Essential Mindsets for Growing Your Professional Services Business demystifies how successful coaches make money while making a difference. The innovative, 10-Step *Seal the Deal* system reveals how to integrate the critical trinity of networking, marketing and sales to find and land the ideal clients who need your genius. Visit the Seal the Deal book website for more information:

http://www.sealthedealbook.com

www.SuziPomerantz.com

About Twitter for Coaches

Here's a sample of what you'll discover:

- A quick start guide explaining how to get set up and how to get into conversations (No technical gobbley gook, just simple English)

- **Avoid an embarrassing mistake by ignoring the first thing "Twitter" asks you to do (It can be like walking into a wedding with no clothes)**

- How to promote your business with class (no one likes the guy constantly pitching, discover my simple mindset for building friendships and promoting at the same time)

- **What you must do to never get overwhelmed by Twitter (if you're afraid of it becoming another email, you'll want to hear this)**

- A simple way to get free tech support (in plain English) who actually know how to solve your problems (Answers for questions like: Why is my computer slowing down?)

- **How to win friends and influence people with Twitter (more importantly, how not to lose friends and business)**

- What you should never tweet (tweet is twitter lingo for talk)

- **How to take a long link and make it shorter (this is critical if you want visitors to your web page because long web addresses can eat up your 140 character limit...fast).**

- How to find the exact people you want to follow

- **One thing you must do before you sign up to make sure people find you easily**

- How to find out what people are saying about you behind your back

- **An easy way to know when you have struck a nerve with your tweets (this is the key to building a following because, people pass on powerful messages and spread your name...for free)**

- How to bond and build trust with complete strangers!

- **My refined system for handling Twitter overload with just 15 minutes of your day, two or three days a week.**

- An easy way to get followers using a secret as old as the bible (You can use this in your everyday business life, too and reap more business)

- **How to pinpoint exactly what to talk about to create more followers with less work**

Get Going on Twitter NOW with the Twitter Tutorial program; a step by step, one-hour mp3 audio download and companion e-book for only **$47**!
www.innovativeleader.com/twitterwithsuzi.htm

About Leading Coaches' Center

The Leading Coaches' Center is a free community where leaders play, learn, contribute and advance our profession together. It's a place where you, as an executive coach, can advance your clients, your business, and your industry in colleagueship with other like-minded colleagues. http://leadingcoachescenter.com to Join.

The Clubhouse is an exclusive, members only club of top executive coaches who want to take their business to the next level while increasing their profound impact on busines leadership worldwide. http://leadingcoachescenter.com/clubhouse